T0380500

MATTHEW ADAMS

Chef Matt's
PLEASING *to the* EYE

ISBN: Softcover   978-1-9845-1468-4
        EBook   978-1-9845-1467-7

Print information available on the last page

Rev. date: 04/10/2018

To order additional copies of this book, contact:
Xlibris
1-888-795-4274
www.Xlibris.com
Orders@Xlibris.com

Dedication

I dedicate my cookbook to my best taste
tester / food critique ever, my mother, the late
Elizabeth Adams and to my father, the late
Wilson Adams whom inspired and taught
me how to cook and also within my own life
helped me in so many ways than anyone else.

Introduction

I took some nutrient, dense foods, fresh veggies, poultry, beef, fish, healthy carbs, and fresh fruits and crafted together some low sodium, mouthwatering, very pleasing to the eye, delicious meals and some sugar-free and fat-free desserts as well as energy drinks to boost your metabolism getting your day started. You will also find my spin on traditional authentic dishes made by my hands only and most importantly a lot of tender loving care which is a major part of my recipes. So thanks for purchasing my cookbook enjoy

The start of my food journey…

Fried tilapia baked sweet potato and broccoli

grilled chicken breast baked sweet potato with green beans

Seafood salad sandwich on torpedo roll with baby spinach leaves and sliced cucumbers

Grilled chicken baked sweet serve with steamed broccoli and cauliflower

Grilled cheese with turkey bacon and sliced tomato served with a tomato soup top with fresh basil and green grapes on the side on whole wheat

Baked salmon white rice string beans

Grilled chicken topped with sautéed Portobello mushroom and tomatoes and a low fat Swiss cheese served with brown rice and blanch broccoli and carrots

Shrimp and linguine in a white wine sauce served with garlic bread

Medium well T-Bone serve with broccoli and mash sauteed onions on the side

Baby back ribs with sweet potato mash with collard greens and seasoned wit smoked turkey butts

Southwest chicken fresh chicken breast marinated in BBQ sauce topped with diced tomatoes and bacon topped with cheddar cheese and scallions

One of my mother's favorite dishes to make porcupines Savory meatballs in a brown gravy served with mashed potatoes and sweet peas

Fresh grilled swordfish topped with a mango reduction served with
a zucchini slaw this this is dedicated to my mother

Banana pudding by Chef Matt the best in all South Jersey
made with Patrick Farms Chessmen cookies

Ground turkey and cheese meatloaf wrapped in bacon served
with sweet potato mash and sauteed zucchini

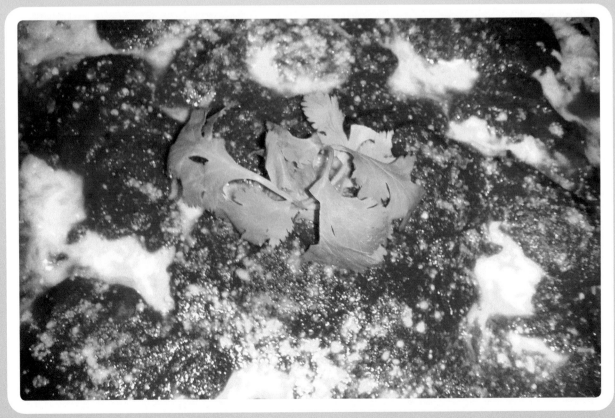

tomato and mozzarella and basil thin crust pizza

grill salmon baked sweet seasoned green beans

grilling shrimp 4 Hickory shrimp brochettes

chicken and shrimp alfredo with sun dried tomatoes

12 russet potatoes baked off cut evenly in half and scoop in mixing bowl along with Parmesan cheese cream cheese sour cream evaporated milk kosher salt white pepper minced onion and chives mixed and stuffed in baker's bag

now potatoes are ready to be stuffed and on their way to be baked a second
time this is why they are called twice baked stuffed potatoes yum!!!

now they are twice baked stuffed potatoes are out of the oven ready to be topped off with some bacon bits... first baking time is 45 minutes to an hour potatoes will be easy to scoop into mixing bowl to prepare your second baking process 25 minutes or until desired Browned

preparing to stuff some rock lobster tail with all lump crab meat

stuffed lobster tails with crab meat

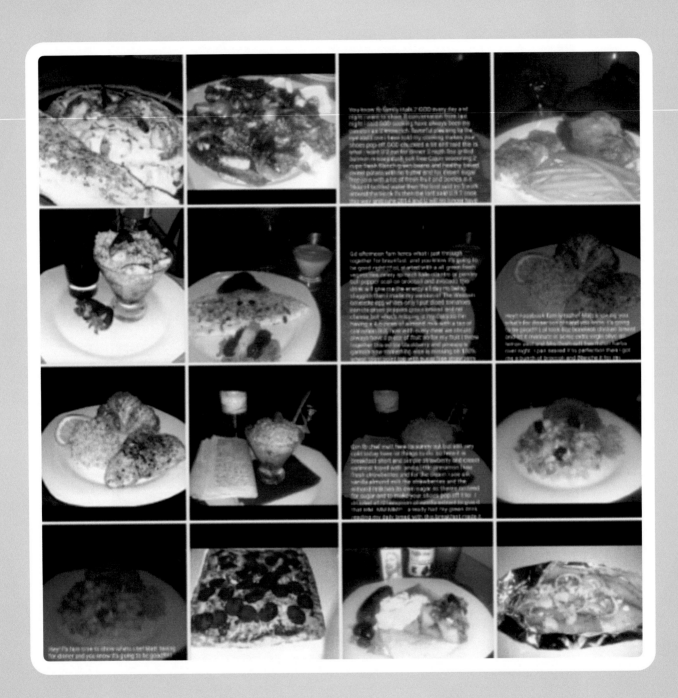

This is what my fridge is going to look like for the next two months....i do this for easy access & freshness I spray my vegetables ... See more

This is what my fridge is going to look like for the next two months....i do this for easy access & freshness I spray my vegetables down once a day with spring water at the same time I'm also rotating I never store in bags(plastic) because it depletes the minerals and nutrients when it's sweats and it deteriorates faster.....very important

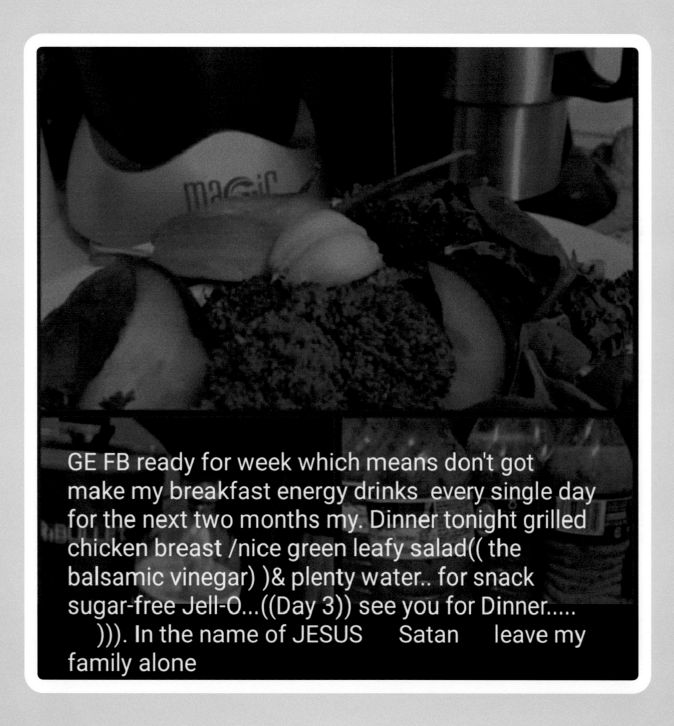

GE FB ready for week which means don't got make my breakfast energy drinks every single day for the next two months my. Dinner tonight grilled chicken breast /nice green leafy salad((the balsamic vinegar))& plenty water.. for snack sugar-free Jell-O...((Day 3)) see you for Dinner.....
))). In the name of JESUS   Satan   leave my family alone

Day (12) Dinner is Ready! Turkey Meatloaf wrapped in Turkey bacon Whipped Sweet Potato & Roasted Yellow Squash..))))). DAMN!!!!

GM fb Day 4 Breakfast Spinach & Mushroom Swiss cheese Omelette with two strips of Turkey bacon 💯 whole-wheat toast Strawberries and Blackberries for my fruit......lol NO 1   WHERE THE   s GOES WHEN THE DOORS R CLOSED BUT GOD   .....

Good Afternoon FB Day (9)This is my Breakfast on the Go..... On My way to Pay Finale Respects to 2 Different Individuals at 2 different locations

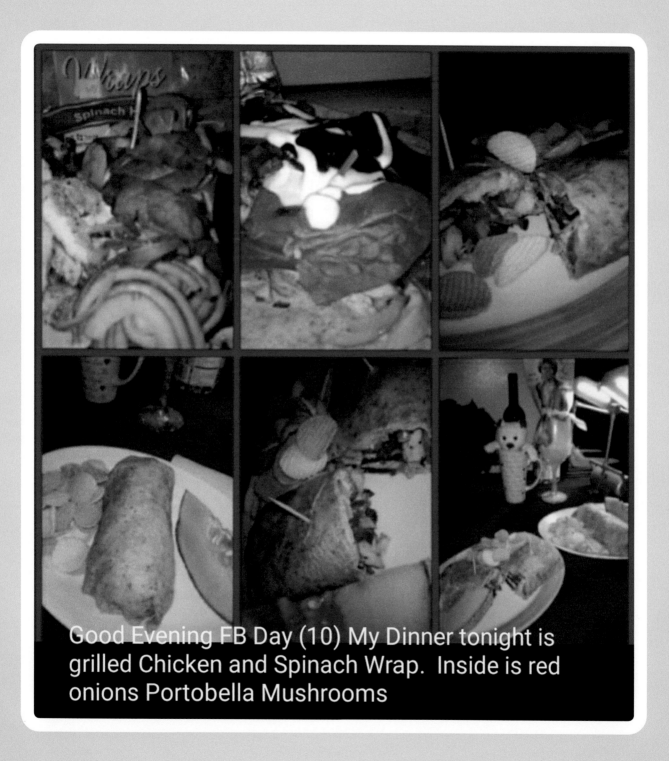

Good Evening FB Day (10) My Dinner tonight is grilled Chicken and Spinach Wrap. Inside is red onions Portobella Mushrooms

Good Evening FB Day(11) for a Healthy Snack got
me some sugar free fat free Jello with some
vanilla Greek yogurt

GE FB Day(17)Dinner Teriyaki grilled Chicken with grilled Broccoli Cauliflower and Red Pepper serving it with whole grain Brown rice and for my Dessert Fat free Sugar free Banana cream pudding with Pistachio nuts... glass of Cabernet Sauvignon...... This Dinner is for you Mom!!!

GE FB Day(19)Dinner real simple Breast Green beans & Sweet & Water.. Wishing all a Good Night

GM! FB Day(21) Breakfast on the Fly...

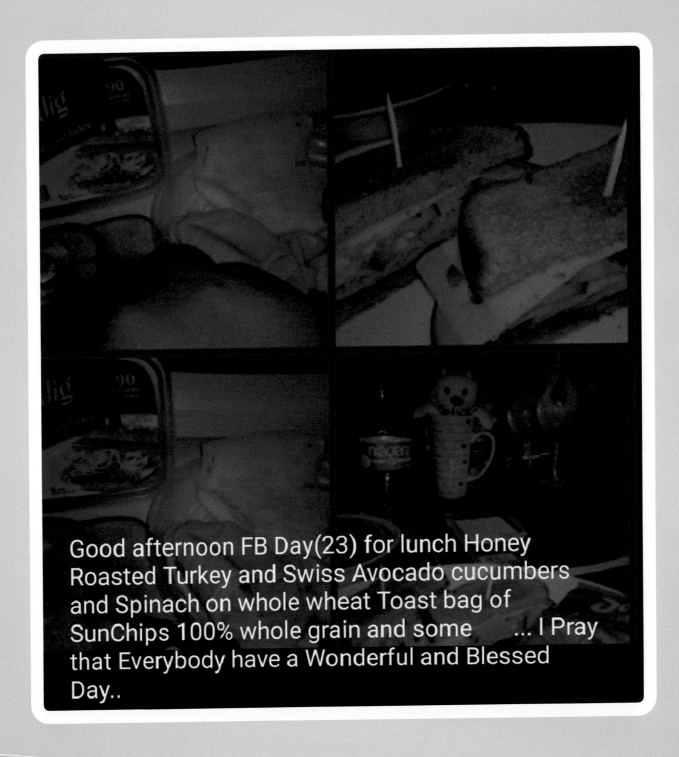

Good afternoon FB Day(23) for lunch Honey
Roasted Turkey and Swiss Avocado cucumbers
and Spinach on whole wheat Toast bag of
SunChips 100% whole grain and some   ... I Pray
that Everybody have a Wonderful and Blessed
Day..

Good Afternoon FB Day (22) lunch low-fat grilled chicken spinach mushrooms tomato Swiss cheese wrap half of green apple and some Greek yogurt..Hope everyone has a Blessed Day

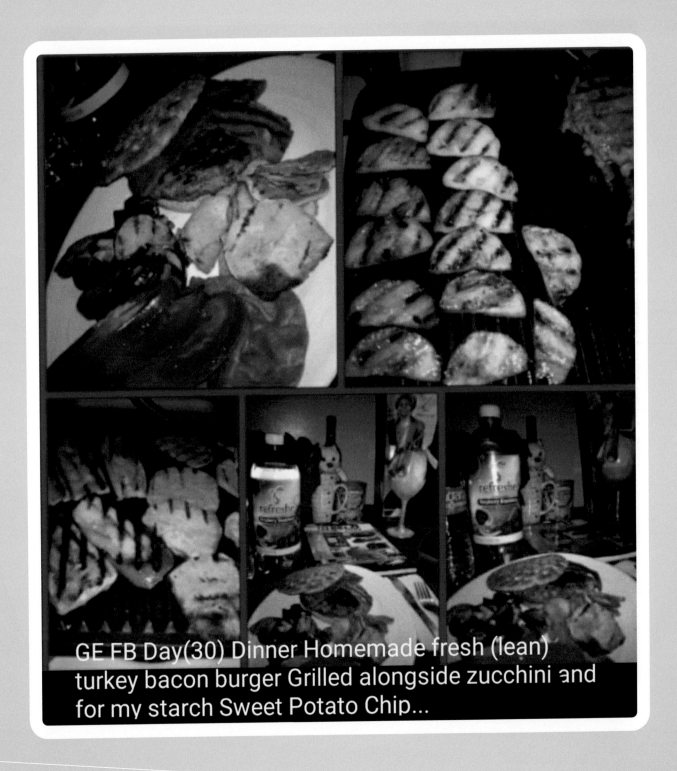

GE FB Day(30) Dinner Homemade fresh (lean) turkey bacon burger Grilled alongside zucchini and for my starch Sweet Potato Chip...

GE FB Day(36) Dinner Crabmeat and Shrimp cooked in a low sodium sauce over Whole Wheat Pasta (gluten free)

Your lunch will be arriving by drone at 1:36 p.m. enjoy so

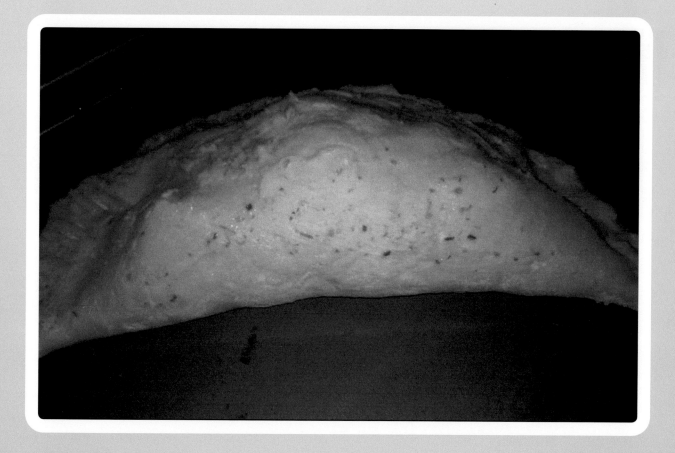

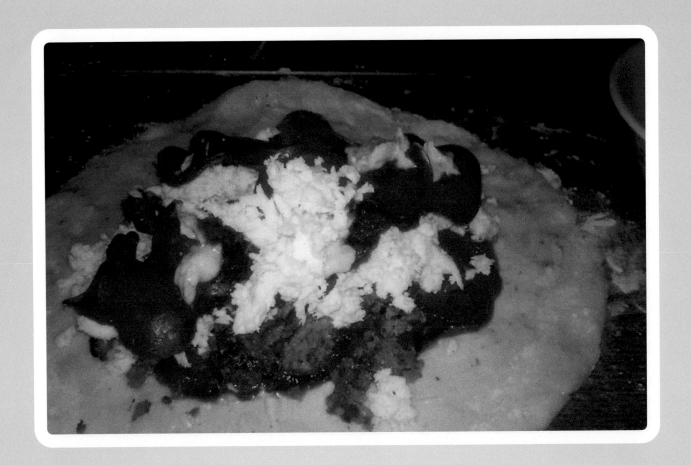

image78

Special thanks to my Savior and Lord Jesus Christ whom giving me the ability and knowledge to create and share my first Cook book(Pleasing To The Eye) I also would like to Thank my Son Eric daughter-in-law Dawn and grandkids Imani Domani Enoni Za'khi Eric Jr

Thank you, my dear readers, for buying this book.
I hope I inspired you with my cooking and I hope
that in your hearts the fire within has been lit.

~~~And you know ... It's gonna be good.~~~
---Matthew Adams

Printed in the United States
By Bookmasters